ACTIVITIES IN FINANCIAL ACCOUNTING
Using Accounting Information in Business Decisions

*(Activities, Cases, Simulations & Projects
for the Accounting Classroom)*

by
Martha S. Doran
San Diego State University

Prentice Hall
Upper Saddle River, NJ 07458

Acquisitions editor: Annie Todd
Assistant editor: Natacha St. Hill
Editorial assistant: Elaine Oyzon-Mast
Marketing manager: Deborah Hoffman Emry
Manufacturing buyer: Alana Zdinak
Cover designer: Suzanne Behnke

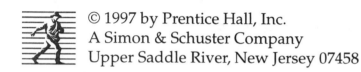
© 1997 by Prentice Hall, Inc.
A Simon & Schuster Company
Upper Saddle River, New Jersey 07458

Printed in the United States of America

10 9 8 7 6 5 4 3 2 1

ISBN 0-13-228966-0

Prentice-Hall International (UK) Limited, *London*
Prentice-Hall of Australia Pty. Limited, *Sydney*
Prentice-Hall Canada Inc., *Toronto*
Prentice-Hall Hispanoamericana, S.A., *Mexico*
Prentice-Hall of India Private Limited, *New Delhi*
Prentice-Hall of Japan, Inc., *Tokyo*
Simon & Schuster Asia Pte. Ltd., *Singapore*
Editora Prentice-Hall do Brasil, Ltda., *Rio de Janeiro*

Table of Contents

To the student...

Regardless of what you think you want to do, accounting will play an important role in whatever you choose. Although you may say "NO! Numbers are NOT my life," we are all influenced, governed, regulated and dependent on numeric measurements. How many of the following questions can you answer in the affirmative?

Have you borrowed or do you plan to borrow money for your education?
Are you receiving or do you plan to receive a paycheck with taxes withheld?
Are you working or do you plan to work for a large corporation?
Are you working or do you plan to work for a small, private company?
Do you plan to start your own business?
Are you raising or do you plan to raise a family?
Are you investing and saving or do you plan to invest and save?
Do you plan to fund your retirement through a pension plan?

Whether you are in the business of getting an education, raising a family, running for president, helping the homeless, making a movie or looking for work, you can make better choices and decisions **when** you learn how to read, measure, analyze, interpret and evaluate accounting information

And that's what this booklet, *Activities in Financial Accounting*, is all about. These activities are designed to help you discover **why** accounting information is so useful, as well as give you a variety of "real-world" situations in which to practice and use your new accounting skills. In addition, most of the activities will also give you an opportunity to practice and improve your writing, speaking and reasoning skills.

If you're saying, "Wait a minute. This is accounting, not an English or speech or logic course," you're not alone, but you **are** in for some changes to your (mis)perceptions. Accounting requires both technical and nontechnical skills. The accounting equation, transactions, financial statements, adjusting entries, accruals, deferrals, ratio analysis ... these are but a few of the important technical aspects of accounting. To be successful, you will need to do more than understand and use the technical skills of accounting. You will need to be able to explain them to your boss, to your employees, to your friends and co-workers, to your family, and, most important, to yourself. Your explanations will require you to use reasoning skills, writing skills and speaking skills. All of these skills work together to make you more productive in this class and in all your endeavors.

The best part of education is to help each person unlock his or her unique talents and to discover how to continue to grow and improve. Grab ahold of the process and hang on to it until you discover how **you** best learn and retain information. This is what college is all about.

WANTED: A Career in Accounting
Activity Overview

Why are we doing this activity?
The purpose of this activity is to help you explore the kinds of skills, knowledge and abilities that today's business world expects to find in qualified job applicants. This activity has you look at the requirements for a job in accounting so you will be aware of the variety of expectations employers may have. This course, in conjunction with all your other courses, is designed to provide you with new skills and knowledge, as well as provide an opportunity for you to use skills and knowledge from other courses.

Content Goals:
* Discover how accounting is used
* Define skills, knowledge and abilities included in this course

Process Goals:
* Explore concept formation
* Transform abstract descriptions into concrete outcomes

Activity Summary:
For starters, you will read and analyze a want ad, which is actually a composite of many different ads from a September 1995 classified section of a western newspaper. You will then try and sort the various job requirements into three broad categories of technical, communication and interpersonal skills. Once you (and your team) have decided which skills are part of each major category, you'll need to come up with descriptions and examples of each skill along with a rationale or reason as to why the skill is needed. Most important, you will also have to define how you would be able to determine if a job applicant actually knew how to perform the skill. Last but not least, you will prepare a list of questions or requirements that you will use to interview prospective applicants who are answering the ad.

Activity Outcome:
When you have completed this activity, you should be able to assume the role of either an interviewer or a job applicant and converse intelligently about the skills, knowledge and abilities needed in accounting. More important, you should be aware of what this course will provide you in terms of new skills as well as opportunities to use prior knowledge. This activity will help you set realistic expectations for the course as well as alert you to what will be expected from your performance.

Class Discussion Notes:

WANTED: A Career in Accounting

ACCOUNTANT

Looking for a highly qualified individual to join our team as a hands-on, self-motivated Acct. Manager/Controller. Must have ability to adapt to a changing work environment and be able to handle both pressure and people. Will work with sales, production and marketing managers to develop projections and budgets. Excellent verbal and written communication skills needed.

Responsibilities include supervising two individuals performing A/R, A/P, Billing and Payroll, preparation and analysis of I/S and B/S, development of accounting procedures, interpretation and analysis of financial information, cost accounting, and budget preparation and analysis. Proficiency in Adv. Lotus 1-2-3 and WordPerfect important.

Position demands excellent technical and interpersonal skills, as well as strong time management skills. We offer a competitive compensation and benefits package. Send résumé and salary requirements to:
> Great Place to Work
> 1234 Main Street
> Real World, USA 98765-4321

WANTED: A Career in Accounting

Directions:

1. Assume you are a member of the Human Resources Department and are in charge of hiring a new accountant for your company. Read the want ad on the previous page that your department placed in Sunday's paper.

2. Identify and list the job requirements described in the ad, using the grid provided below.

3. Sort and classify the job requirements into one of the three major categories shown in the grid (i.e., Technical, Communication, Interpersonal), by placing an "X" in the best grid category.

4. Discuss and evaluate your list with your team or class. Make any changes agreed upon in the larger discussion in the new space provided for you under GROUP DISCUSSIONS.

5. Analyze each job requirement and describe WHAT the skill is, WHY the skill is needed, and HOW you could determine if someone possessed that skill. Use the worksheet provided on the next page.

6. Prepare a list of interview questions or requirements and be prepared to assume the role of either an interviewer or a job applicant. Use the worksheet provided on the last page of this activity.

INDIVIDUAL RESPONSES:

Major Skills: Job Requirements	Technical	Communication	Interpersonal
1			
2			
3			
4			
5			
6			
7			
8			
9			
10			

WANTED: A Career in Accounting

GROUP DISCUSSIONS:

Major Skills: Job Requirements	Technical	Communication	Interpersonal
1			
2			
3			
4			
5			
6			
7			
8			
9			
10			

SKILL ANALYSIS WORKSHEET:

Major Skills:	WHAT is the skill?	WHY is it needed?	HOW do you know someone has it?
1			
2			
3			
4			
5			
6			
7			
8			
9			
10			

NAME:_____

WANTED: A Career in Accounting

Use this page to prepare a list of interview questions or requirements you will use to satisfy yourself that the job applicant is well qualified and right for the job. Be prepared to assume either the role of interviewer or applicant. In other words, make sure you know the kinds of answers or results you are seeking with each of the questions or requirements you create. Some "Reasoning Tips" are provided in Appendix A, p.71, to help you review your critical thinking skills.

1.

2.

3.

4.

5.

6.

7.

8.

PIZZA! PIZZA!
Activity Overview

Why are we doing this activity?

The purpose of this activity is to help you explore the kinds of accounting information that are available to decision makers and why such information is necessary. This activity places you in the role of an entrepreneur who is interested in purchasing a pizza shop. This is an important decision that will require you to comprehend what information is quantitative and relevant to this decision and why.

Content Goals:
* Discover how accounting is used
* Distinguish between quantitative and qualitative information

Process Goals:
* Explain WHAT and WHY
* Developing deep questioning techniques

Activity Summary:

You will assume the role of a would-be business owner, who has very little information with which to decide whether to buy a pizza parlor. The good news is that you can ask 10 questions before you make this momentous decision. The dilemma is ... which 10 questions are the best ones to ask?

Activity Outcome:

When you have completed this activity, you should be able to explain WHAT you need to know (the 10 questions) and also WHY each question will help you make a good decision. This activity will help you comprehend how accounting information can be used, and to discern which questions accounting information can and cannot answer. You will also practice your impromptu speaking skills and develop your reasoning skills in deep questioning.

Class Discussion Notes:

PIZZA! PIZZA!

For quite some time you have been dreaming about starting your own business ... and it looks like opportunity has knocked! The local pizza parlor is up for sale. It's located just a few blocks from the house where you grew up. And the delicious tastes and smells of this pizza parlor have been part of your growing up. The good news is that you have obtained the company's income statement for the current year and it shows a $75,000 net profit after taxes. The bad news is this income statement is the ONLY statement ever prepared for the pizza parlor. You want to present your best offer to purchase the pizza parlor from the current owner, and time is of the essence. You can ask ONLY 10 questions to prepare your offer.

Directions:

1. Brainstorm a list of as many questions you can think of to help you make your best offer for the pizza parlor. Jot down WHY each question will help you. Use the space provided below.

2. Use your first list to rank the most important questions and to narrow your list to 10 questions. Check to see if some of your questions fall into the same categories. Are two or more questions answering the same WHY? Do you need both questions?

3. Prepare a final list of your top 10 questions, along with the reason WHY each question will help you make an offer. Be ready to briefly share your top three questions along with the amount of your offer for the pizza parlor. Use the worksheet provided on the next page.

BRAINSTORMING QUESTIONS: **WHY:**   **RANK**

NAME:_____

PIZZA! PIZZA!

Use this worksheet to list your top 10 questions and tell why each question will help you make your best offer for the pizza parlor. List the amount you would offer to buy the business.

Top 10 Questions	Why this information is important:
1.	
2.	
3.	
4.	
5.	
6.	
7.	
8.	
9.	
10.	

Amount of your OFFER to purchase this business: $_____

Compu-Shack: Using Financial Printouts
Activity Overview

Why are we doing this activity?

The purpose of this activity is to give you experience in reading and using computer printouts of financial reporting. Most businesses use computer software to record their economic transactions. Although every software package is unique, you will also discover many similarities. This activity is designed to have you explore and comprehend a company's financial transactions when presented as a computerized set of reports.

Content Goal:
* Read and analyze the basic steps of the accounting cycle

Process Goal:
* Recognize similarities in the reporting process, independent of the reporting medium

Activity Summary:

Using computer printouts for Compu-Shack, you will answer eight questions about the company's operations. Your answers will need to include BOTH a factual response AND an explanation of "how" or "where" you discovered each answer.

Activity Outcome:

When you have completed this activity, you should be able to find specific information about a company by reading its computer printouts. Additionally, you should recognize economic transactions and their effect on the accounting equation. You should also become aware of some of the limitations of accounting information.

Class Discussion Notes:

NAME:_____

Compu-Shack: Using Financial Printouts

Directions:

1. Read the computer printouts for Compu-Shack, starting on page 15. Then complete the worksheet below. You need to provide BOTH a factual answer to each question <u>AND</u> a description of "how" or "where" you found your answer.

<u>QUESTION:</u>	<u>ANSWER:</u>	<u>HOW/WHERE?</u>

1. What kind of business entity is Compu-Shack?

2. How long has Compu-Shack been in business?

3. How much money did Compu-Shack start and end September with?

4. Where did it get its cash?

5. Where did it spend its cash?

6. Use the accounting equation to represent Compu-Shack.

$$A \quad = \quad L \quad + \quad OE$$
$$\underline{\quad\quad} = \underline{\quad\quad} + \underline{\quad\quad}$$

7. What was Compu-Shack's bottom line for September?

8. How knowledgeable and experienced are the owners of Compu-Shack?

Compu-Shack: The Case of the Missing Files
Activity Overview

Why are we doing this activity?

The purpose of this activity is to help you translate accounting entries into English, as well as describe and comprehend the impact these adjustments have on the financial reports, transactions, and <u>why</u> each adjustment is being made. Since most technical accounting procedures are now performed by computers, it is extremely important for users of accounting information to understand what is being done by a computer and why.

Content Goals:
* Describe economic events underlying accounting adjustments
* Recognize the impact an adjustment has
* Explain the business logic for making each adjustment

Process Goals:
* Comprehend the process of reading financial records to discover economic meaning from the results

Activity Summary:

You will play the role of an accounting detective of sorts and help the owners of Compu-Shack "reconstruct" missing journal entries. The records may have been misfiled or destroyed, but in either case you have been asked to come to the rescue. This case is very similar to what accountants often do for their clients, so the steps (process) are important. The first task asks you to summarize what's happened so far. Next you are asked to think up a list of possible adjustments to be made. Last, you are asked to actually reconstruct the entries based on the printouts you have.

Activity Outcome:

When you have completed this activity, you should be able to describe and explain accounting adjustments made to financial reports by reading the company's computer printouts. Additionally, you should recognize how adjustments affect the financial statements and be able to discern the differences between transactions and adjustments.

Class Discussion Notes:

Compu-Shack: The Case of the Missing Files

Two of your good friends need your help. They recently started a new business called Compu-Shack. But their trusty accountant left the country (for Tahiti, they think) and they can't find all of the accounting records. They have located an adjusted trial balance and the general ledger but cannot find the listing of the adjusting journal entries the accountant made for them. The adjusted trial balance shows that the adjustments were correctly posted, but they also want to make sure they have perfect documentation of the entries. You've agreed to help reconstruct the entries.

Directions:

1. Read through the computer reports for Compu-Shack (pages 16-22). Use the description of the transactions listed in the General Journal to help you write a brief, one-paragraph summary of what business activity took place in September (BEFORE any adjustments). Space is provided below for your paragraph summary.

2. Next, jot down a list of possible transactions that may need to be adjusted at the end of September. Think of this step as preparing a checklist of transactions you want to analyze for possible adjustment. Space is also provided for this checklist below.

3. Read through the Adjusted Trial Balance and "reconstruct" the adjusting journal entries (AJEs) made for Compu-Shack. Use the worksheet provided on the next page.

4. For each entry, (a) write a description of what was accomplished by the entry, (b) describe the impact the entry had on the balance sheet and income statement, and (c) describe why the entry was made.

Paragraph Summary (for #1):

Checklist of Transactions to Adjust (for #2):

NAME:_____

Compu-Shack: The Case of the Missing Files

Directions:
Use the worksheets on this page and the next one to complete steps 3 and 4, listed under "Directions" on the previous page. Reconstruct the six journal entries posted on Compu-Shack's Adjusted Trial Balance. For each AJE, provide the entry, a description of the entry, the impact on the balance sheet and income statement, and why the adjustment needed to be made. The first one is done as an example for you.

AJE #1:

Cost of sales	#451	$34,672.00
Merchandise Inventory	#131	$34,672.00

Description: To record cost of merchandise sold based on a periodic inventory count at the end of September.

Impact: Decreased assets (inventory) on the balance sheet and decreased net income (or increased expenses) on the income statement.

Why: Need to recognize the costs of assets (inventory) sold as an expense on the income statement to correctly match the costs with the revenue produced. No future benefit to the assets "used" (sold), so the expired cost is transferred to the income statement as an expense.

AJE #2:
Description:

Impact:

Why:

NAME:_____

Compu-Shack: The Case of the Missing Files

AJE #3:
Description:

Impact:

Why:

AJE #4:
Description:

Impact:

Why:

AJE #5:
Description:

Impact:

Why:

AJE #6:
Description:

Impact:

Why:

Compu-Shack
A California Corporation
Working Trial Balance
For the period ending September 30, 1995

Prepared by: _____

Reviewed by: _____

Page 1

Account #	Account Name	Unadjusted Trial Balance Dr/(Cr)	Ref #	Adjustment Dr/(Cr)	Balance Sheet Dr	Cr
101	Petty Cash	125.00			125.00	
102	Cash In Bank	87,285.00			87,285.00	
121	Account Receivable	10,215.00			10,215.00	
131	Merchandise Inventory	170,400.00	AJE-1	(34,672.00)	135,728.00	
151	Furniture & Fixtures	7,200.00			7,200.00	
161	Acumulated Depreciation		AJE-3	(60.00)		60.00
171	Prepaid Insurance	2,100.00	AJE-5	(175.00)	1,925.00	
172	Prepaid Rent	1,350.00			1,350.00	
201	Accounts Payable	(83,950.00)	AJE-6	(205.00)		84,155.00
205	Bank Loan Payable	(100,000.00)				100,000.00
251	Accured Wages Payable		AJE-2	(400.00)		400.00
255	Interest Payable		AJE-4	(1,250.00)		1,250.00
259	Utilities Payable					
301	Common Stock	(50,000.00)				50,000.00
395	Retained Earnings					
		44,725.00		(36,762.00)	243,828.00	235,865.00
396	Profit & Loss Summary					7,963.00
		44,725.00		(36,762.00)	243,828.00	243,828.00

Compu-Shack
A California Corporation
Working Trial Balance
For the period ending September 30, 1995

Prepared by: _____

Reviewed by: _____

Page 2

Account #	Account Name	Unadjusted Trial Balance Dr/(Cr)	Ref #	Adjustment Dr/(Cr)	Income Statement Dr	Income Statement Cr
401	Sales	(50,000.00)				50,000.00
451	Cost of Sales		AJE-1	34,672.00	34,672.00	
501	Advertising Expense	1,200.00			1,200.00	
515	Depreciation Expense		AJE-3	60.00	60.00	
530	Insurance Expense		AJE-5	175.00	175.00	
531	Interest Expense		AJE-4	1,250.00	1,250.00	
551	Office Supplies Expense	1,000.00			1,000.00	
571	Rent Expense	1,350.00			1,350.00	
581	Utilities Expense	250.00	AJE-6	205.00	455.00	
591	Wages Expense	1,475.00	AJE-2	400.00	1,875.00	
695	Miscellaneous Expenses					
		(44,725.00)		36,762.00	42,037.00	50,000.00
	Profit & Loss Summary				7,963.00	
		(44,725.00)		36,762.00	50,000.00	50,000.00

Compu-Shack
A California Corporation
General Journal Entries
For the period ending September 30, 1995

Prepared by: _____

Reviewed by: _____

Page 1

Account #	Account Name		Debit	Credit
		GJE-1		
131	Merchandise Inventory		125,000.00	
201	Accounts Payable			125,000.00
	(To record purchases of merchandise on account)			
		GJE-2		
121	Accounts Receivable		13,500.00	
401	Sales			13,500.00
	(To record credit sales for September)			
		GJE-3		
131	Merchandise Inventory		45,400.00	
201	Accounts Payable			45,400.00
	(To record purchases on account for inventory)			
		GJE-4		
151	Furniture & Fixtures		1,000.00	
201	Accounts Payable			1,000.00
	(To record balance due on sign purchase, due 12/31)			
			184,900.00	184,900.00

```
   123-01                          Compu-Shack
                             A California Corporation
   06/15/96                  General Ledger Listing - Detail
   12:18 PM               For the period ended September 30, 1995              Page   1

   Acct/Date     Description                 Source/Ref              Amount
   -----------------------------------------------------------------------------------
   101          Petty Cash                                               0.00    *
     09/22/95     Cash                        C/D 109                  125.00
                                                                       125.00   **


   102          Cash in Bank                                             0.00    *
     09/27/95     Cash                        C/D POST          (102,500.00)
     09/29/95     Cash Receipts Summary       C/R POST           189,785.00
                                                                  87,285.00   **


   121          Accounts Receivable                                      0.00    *
     09/24/95     Payments from Customers      C/R 4             (3,285.00)
     09/30/95     Accounts Receivable          GJE 2             13,500.00
                                                                  10,215.00   **


   131          Merchandise Inventory                                    0.00    *
     09/30/95     Merchandise Inventory        AJE 1            (34,672.00)
     09/30/95     Merchandise Inventory        GJE 1            125,000.00
     09/30/95     Merchandise Inventory        GJE 3             45,400.00
                                                                 135,728.00   **


   151          Furniture and Fixtures                                   0.00    *
     09/01/95     Staples                      C/D 102            5,600.00
     09/27/95     Signs 'R Us, Inc.            C/D 112              600.00
     09/30/95     Furniture and Fixtures       GJE 4             1,000.00
                                                                   7,200.00   **


   161          Accumulated Depreciation                                 0.00    *
     09/30/95     Accumulated Depreciation     AJE 3               (60.00)
                                                                     (60.00)  **


   171          Prepaid Insurance                                        0.00    *
     09/27/95     State Farm Insurance         C/D 111            2,100.00
     09/30/95     Prepaid Insurance            AJE 5               (175.00)
                                                                   1,925.00   **


   172          Prepaid Rent                                             0.00    *
     09/27/95     Century 21 Realty Mngt       C/D 110            1,350.00
                                                                   1,350.00   **


   201          Accounts Payable                                         0.00    *
     09/01/95     Bank Loan                    C/R 1          (100,000.00)
     09/15/95     Intel                        C/D 107           87,450.00
     09/30/95     Accounts Payable             AJE 6             (205.00)
     09/30/95     Accounts Payable             GJE 1         (125,000.00)
     09/30/95     Accounts Payable             GJE 3          (45,400.00)
     09/30/95     Accounts Payable             GJE 4           (1,000.00)
                                                                (184,155.00) **


   205          Bank Loan Payable                                        0.00    *
                                                                       0.00   **
```

```
123-01                      Compu-Shack
                        A California Corporation
06/15/96               General Ledger Listing - Detail
12:18 PM           For the period ended September 30, 1995          Page    2

  Acct/Date      Description                Source/Ref           Amount
------------------------------------------------------------------------------

  251          Accrued Wages Payable                                0.00   *
    09/30/95     Accrued Wages Payable      AJE 2                 (400.00)
                                                                 (400.00) **

  255          Interest Payable                                    0.00   *
    09/30/95     Interest Payable           AJE 4               (1,250.00)
                                                               (1,250.00) **

  259          Utilities Payable                                    0.00   *
                                                                    0.00  **

  301          Common Stock                                         0.00   *
    09/01/95     Stock for Cash Contrib.    C/R 2              (50,000.00)
                                                              (50,000.00) **

  395          Retained Earnings                                    0.00   *
                                                                    0.00  **

  396          P&L Summary                                          0.00   *
                                                                    0.00  **

  401          Sales                                                0.00   *
    09/24/95     Cash Sales                 C/R 3              (36,500.00)
    09/30/95     Sales                      GJE 2              (13,500.00)
                                                              (50,000.00) **

  451          Cost of Sales                                        0.00   *
    09/30/95     Cost of Sales              AJE 1               34,672.00
                                                               34,672.00  **

  501          Advertising Expense                                  0.00   *
    09/05/95     Gallagher & Co.            C/D 103             1,200.00
                                                                1,200.00  **

  515          Depreciation Expense                                 0.00   *
    09/30/95     Depreciation Expense       AJE 3                  60.00
                                                                   60.00  **

  530          Insurance Expense                                    0.00   *
    09/30/95     Insurance Expense          AJE 5                 175.00
                                                                  175.00  **

  531          Interest Expense                                     0.00   *
    09/30/95     Interest Expense           AJE 4               1,250.00
                                                                1,250.00  **

  551          Office Supplies Expense                              0.00   *
    09/09/95     Office Depot               C/D 105             1,000.00
                                                                1,000.00  **
```

```
    123-01                          Compu-Shack
                             A California Corporation
  06/15/96                  General Ledger Listing - Detail
  12:18 PM              For the period ended September 30, 1995          Page    3

  Acct/Date    Description               Source/Ref          Amount
  ------------------------------------------------------------------------------
  571          Rent Expense                                        0.00  *
    09/01/95     Century 21 Realty Mngt    C/D 101           1,350.00
                                                             1,350.00  **

  581          Utilities Expense                                   0.00  *
    09/15/95     Pacific Gas & Power       C/D 106             250.00
    09/30/95     Utilities Expense         AJE 6               205.00
                                                               455.00  **

  591          Wages Expense                                       0.00  *
    09/09/95     Accountemps               C/D 104             850.00
    09/15/95     Accountemps               C/D 108             625.00
    09/30/95     Wages Expense             AJE 2               400.00
                                                             1,875.00  **

  695          Miscellaneous                                       0.00  *
                                                                   0.00  **
                                                         ----------------

                           Total Debits                    513,947.00
                           Total Credits                   513,947.00
                           Difference                            0.00  **
```

```
   123-01                        Compu-Shack
                            A California Corporation
  06/15/96                    Cash Disbursements
  12:23 PM          For the period ended September 30, 1995            Page    1

    Account #      Date      Description          Reference      Amount
  ---------------------------------------------------------------------------------

         571   09/01/95  Century 21 Realty Mngt       101         1,350.00

         151   09/01/95  Staples                      102         5,600.00

         501   09/05/95  Gallagher & Co.              103         1,200.00

         591   09/09/95  Accountemps                  104           850.00

         551   09/09/95  Office Depot                 105         1,000.00

         581   09/15/95  Pacific Gas & Power          106           250.00

         201   09/15/95  Intel                        107        87,450.00

         591   09/15/95  Accountemps                  108           625.00

         101   09/22/95  Cash                         109           125.00

         172   09/27/95  Century 21 Realty Mngt       110         1,350.00

         171   09/27/95  State Farm Insurance         111         2,100.00

         151   09/27/95  Signs 'R Us, Inc.            112           600.00

         102   09/27/95  Cash                        POST      (102,500.00)
                                                              ----------------
                                           Total Debits       102,500.00
                                           Total Credits      102,500.00
  ---------------------------------------------------------------------------------

   123-01                        Compu-Shack
                            A California Corporation
  06/15/96                      Cash Receipts
  12:23 PM          For the period ended September 30, 1995            Page    1

    Account #      Date      Description          Reference      Amount
  ---------------------------------------------------------------------------------

         201   09/01/95  Bank Loan                      1      (100,000.00)

         301   09/01/95  Stock for Cash Contrib.        2       (50,000.00)

         401   09/24/95  Cash Sales                     3       (36,500.00)

         121   09/24/95  Payments from Customers        4        (3,285.00)

         102   09/29/95  Cash Receipts Summary       POST       189,785.00
                                                              ----------------
                                           Total Debits        189,785.00
                                           Total Credits       189,785.00
```

Kmart's Blue Light Specials: Keeping the Creditors Happy
Activity Overview

Why are we doing this activity?

The purpose of this activity is to enable you to apply new vocabulary and accounting concepts concerning liabilities to a specific financial announcement concerning Kmart. You will need to utilize new accounting comprehension as well as reading and logic skills.

Content Goals:
* Interpret new accounting vocabulary regarding debt
* Apply new concepts in "real world" analysis of article on Kmart

Process Goal:
* Read business news for meaning

Activity Summary:

In this activity, you will individually read a short newspaper article concerning Kmart's new debt agreements. Then you will interpret three specific quotations from the article, paying special attention to the accounting terminology of debt (liabilities). You will then trade papers with a teammate and check each other's work.

Activity Outcome:

When you have completed this activity, you should be more experienced in reading articles for business meaning. You should also be better able to distinguish synonymous terms (debt, creditors, etc.) from related terms (debt, equity).

Class Discussion Notes:

NAME:_____

Kmart's Blue Light Specials

Directions:

1. Read the article "Kmart seals debt pact; stock leaps" on page 28.

2. Explain in your own words (not accounting jargon)
   (a.) what is meant by each quotation; and

   (b.) relate it to Kmart's liability section and stockholder's equity section.

(NOTE: The first one is done as an example.)

3. Exchange papers with a team member and make an "X" next to any response that does not agree with yours.

4. Return each other's papers and discuss any areas with an "X."

==

Quotations:

1. " .... it had eliminated its quarterly dividend and reached an agreement in principle to extend terms on $3 billion in bank debt."

   (a) *Kmart won't pay a dividend this quarter and has gotten the bank to agree to a longer length of time to pay back its debt, but no official agreement has been signed (just "in principle").*

   (b) *Change to liability section MAY show debt reclassified as long-term; new terms MAY be disclosed in footnotes or in Management Report but not in numbers; no equity changes.*

2. "Holders of $54.8 million in real estate debt agreed to scrap a provision allowing them to demand immediate repayment if Kmart's debt was downgraded to junk-bond status."

   (a)

   (b)

NAME:_____
Kmart's Blue Light Specials

Quotations (continued):

3. " ... by removing the threat that a mountain of bills would come due when the troubled retailer could not afford to pay."

   (a)

   (b)

4. " Kmart is expecting to use proceeds from the sale of as much as $1.2 billion in debt or stock to pay down some of its bank debt."

   (a)

   (b)

Kmart's News: Debt Affects Equity?
Activity Overview

Why are we doing this activity?

The purpose of this activity is to help you synthesize your new knowledge of debt and equity in the context of a publicly traded corporation (Kmart). These two methods for financing have similarities and differences, as well as advantages and disadvantages. The numbers (or accounting) are just the starting point in evaluating financial information and making good decisions. The skill of using your knowledge <u>in context</u> is the most important aspect of your education.

Content Goals:
* Compare and contrast debt vs. equity
* Infer and reason through strengths and weaknesses of debt/equity as applied to Kmart

Process Goals:
* Utilize the business reference section of library

Activity Summary:

For starters, you will read a newspaper article on Kmart and complete a brief worksheet of terms and quotations to help you comprehend accounting and business terminology in context. You will then need to locate a copy of the 12/31/95 financial statement (in the library) and prepare a worksheet of debt and equity ratios. Based on your findings, you will then prepare a plan to help Kmart "get its house in order."

Activity Outcome:

When you have completed this activity, you should be able to identify specific strengths and weaknesses in both debt and equity financing as it relates to Kmart. You will also have more experience in effectively communicating action plans.

Class Discussion Notes:

Kmart's News: Debt Affects Equity?

Directions:

1. Read the article "Kmart seals debt pact; stock leaps," on page 28.

2. Complete the worksheet below of quotations and questions from the article by explaining in non accounting terms what is being reported.

3. Locate a copy of the 12/31/95 annual report and financial statements from the business reference section of the library. Use these statements to complete the debt and equity ratio worksheet on the next page.

4. Based on your findings in the ratio analyses, your knowledge of accounting, and your reading of the financial statements, prepare a memo outlining a plan of your recommendations to help Kmart "get its house in order."

Reading for Meaning:

1. Explain "an accord with creditors that eases its financial pain but does not cure its problems."

2. Why aren't the problems cured?

3. Why did Kmart's stock leap?

4. Explain "jump-start its chain of 2,100 discount stores after three years of sliding profits and shrinking market share."

5. Do accountants have the answer to #4? Explain.

NAME:_____

Kmart's News: Debt Affects Equity?

Use this worksheet to complete the debt and equity ratios listed below for Kmart, as of December 31, 1995. These ratios should assist your analysis and recommendations to help Kmart "get its house in order."

Debt and Equity Ratios:

1. Debt to Equity Ratio

2. Times Interest Earned:

$$\frac{EBIT}{\text{Interest on L/T Debt}}$$

3. Return on Equity:

$$\frac{\text{Net Income}}{\text{Common Equity}}$$

4. Earnings per Share (EPS)

5. Price to Earnings:

$$\frac{\text{Market Price (per common)}}{\text{Earnings per Share (EPS)}}$$

6. Market to Book:

$$\frac{\text{Market Price (per common)}}{\text{Book Value (per common) *}}$$

* (common equity/# of common shares outstanding)

Kmart seals debt pact; stock leaps

(taken from San Diego Union-Tribune, December 22, 1995, p.C-2)

Accord with creditors eases firms problems, but doesn't cure them

By MELISSA GEORGE
Reuters

CHICAGO -- Kmart Corp.'s stock jumped more than 25 percent yesterday, a day after it unveiled an accord with creditors that eases its financial pain but doesn't cure its problems.

The retailer said late Wednesday it had eliminated its quarterly dividend and reached an agreement in principle to extend terms on a $3 billion bank debt.

The retailer also said holders of $548 million in real estate debt agreed to scrap a provision allowing them to demand immediate repayment if Kmart's debt was downgraded to junk bond status.

Kmart's shares rose $1.62 1/2 to $7.62 1/2 on the NYSE, where it was the most heavily traded stock.

The deal pulls Kmart back from the brink of bankruptcy, industry analysts said, by removing the threat that a mountain of bills would come due when the troubled retailer could not afford to pay.

"They've clearly bought time to work on obvious operational and competitive issues facing them," said G. Strachan of Goldman, Sachs & Co.

The deal with creditors was warmly welcomed by Kmart's suppliers, who had grown nervous that the company would follow the long string of discounters that have filed for Chapter 11 protection this year.

"We're still careful about Kmart, but we're very happy" with its agreement, said an executive at one large NY firm which guarantees payment to suppliers on behalf of retailers.

But Kmart has merely postponed its problems, experts said. The company still faces a daunting task of stabilizing its financial structures by 1997 when $3.7 billion in debt is due.

"Longer term doesn't solve anything," said one Wall Street analyst who asked not to be identified.

A rebound at Kmart ultimately hinges on its ability to jump-start its chain of 2,100 discount stores after three years of sliding profits and shrinking market share, analysts said.

Yesterday, Moody's Investor Service cut Kmart's debt rating to one notch above junk-bond status and kept it under review for another possible downgrade. Standard & Poor's is considering a downgrade.

Soft sales among retailers this holiday season will only make it more difficult for Kmart's new Chairman and CEO, Floyd Hall, to turn around the struggling discounter, Moody's said.

Kmart spokesman Robert Burton said concerns about talks with creditors were overblown, and the company was as devoted as ever to fixing its operations woes. "The real issue is turning around Kmart," Burton said.

Next year, Kmart is expected to use proceeds from the sale of as much as $1.2 billion in debt or stock to pay down some of its bank debt.

This strategy might just replace new debt for old, analysts said. The company now needs to get its house in order to pull off healthy sales increases next holiday season.

Changes in Financial Statements: Read Me a Story
Activity Overview

Why are we doing this activity?

The purpose of this activity is to help you become better readers of financial statements. Although financial statements are presented as numbers, the changes in the numbers from one statement to the next tell the story of a business's economic events (happenings). This activity will help you practice the skill of reading numbers and then translating what you read in to words ... the business story that can't be hidden.

Content Goals:
* Identify changes in a series of balance sheets
* Interpret economic meaning from changes in the numbers

Process Goal:
* Increase written communication skills

Activity Summary:

This activity presents a series of four "snapshots" of a newly formed business called Romance, Inc. (a service giving gondola rides on the river). After reading each statement (snapshot), you need to explain both the numeric changes in the statements and their business "story" (what economic event happened to create the numeric changes).

Activity Outcome:

When you have completed this activity, you should be able to explain economic events by reading and analyzing a series of financial statements.

Class Discussion Notes:

NAME:_____

Changes in Financial Statements: Read Me a Story

Directions:

1. Read each Balance Sheet (snapshot), of Romance, Inc. and then provide a written explanation of (a) the numeric changes and (b) the economic event (the story). Each Balance Sheet is progressive, so you need to look at the prior statement to determine changes in the next statement. NOTE: The business began operations on January 2, 1996, with no assets, liabilities or equity. The boat was purchased. **The first one is done as an example.**

Romance, Inc.
Balance Sheet
January 4, 1996

#1	Cash	50,000			
	Fixed Assets (boat)	50,000	Common Stock	100,000
	TOTAL ASSETS	$100,000	TOTAL EQUITY	$100,000

(a) Assets (cash 50,000 + boat 50,000) increased by 100,000
     Equity (common stock) increased by 100,000

$$A = L + OE$$
$$100,000 = 0 + 100,000$$

(b) The owner(s) contributed 100,000 cash in exchange for 100,000 in common stock and then purchased a boat for 50,000 cash.

Romance, Inc.
Balance Sheet
January 11, 1996

#2	Cash	48,000	Acct Payable	3,000
	Prepaid Rent	2,000		
	Fixed Assets (canopy)	3,000		
	Fixed Assets (boat)	50,000	Common Stock	100,000
	TOTAL ASSETS	$103,000	TOTAL LIAB. & EQUITY	$103,000

(a)

(b)

NAME:_____
Changes in Financial Statements: Read Me a Story

Romance, Inc.
Balance Sheet
January 18, 1996

#3

Cash	48,000	Acct Payable	3,000
Accts Receivable	5,000		
Prepaid Rent	2,000		
Fixed Assets (canopy)	3,000	Common Stock	100,000
Fixed Assets (boat)	50,000	Retained Earnings	5,000
TOTAL ASSETS	$108,000	TOTAL LIAB. & EQUITY	$108,000

(a)

(b)

Romance, Inc.
Balance Sheet
January 25, 1996

#4

Cash	50,000	Acct Payable	3,000
Accts Receivable	3,000		
Prepaid Rent	2,000		
Fixed Assets (canopy)	3,000	Common Stock	100,000
Fixed Assets (boat)	50,000	Retained Earnings	5,000
TOTAL ASSETS	$108,000	TOTAL LIAB. & EQUITY	$108,000

(a)

(b)

Changes in Financial Statements: Pulling It All Together
Activity Overview

Why are we doing this activity?
> The purpose of this activity is to help you synthesize the skills of reading, interpreting and then being able to record economic events using accounting techniques. This activity combines three key components of WHAT, WHY and HOW ... WHAT events took place in the company, WHY the event was recorded and HOW it was recorded.

Content Goals:
* Identify WHAT took place
* Explain WHY the event was recorded
* Demonstrate HOW the event was recorded

Process Goal:
* Synthesize technical skills, reasoning skills and communication skills

Activity Summary:
> This is a comprehensive activity presenting eight snapshots of a newly formed company: Romance, Inc., a service providing gondola rides on the river. After reading each statement, you need to identify numeric changes to the accounting equation (WHAT), explain the economic transaction that caused the changes to take place (WHY) and then provide the necessary journal entry to record the event or adjustment (HOW).

Activity Outcome:
> When you have completed this activity, you should be able to identify changes in financial statements, explain the concepts as they relate to the accounting equation, and be able to use bookkeeping techniques to record transactions and adjustments.

Class Discussion Notes:

NAME:_____

Changes in Financial Statements: Pulling It All Together

Directions:

1. Read each Balance Sheet (snapshot), of Romance, Inc., and then provide a written explanation of (a) the numeric changes, (b) the economic event (the story) and (c) the journal entry or entries to record the event. Each Balance Sheet is progressive, so you need to look at the prior statement to determine changes in the next statement. NOTE: The business began operations on January 2, 1996, with no assets, liabilities or equity. The boat was purchased. **The first one is done as an example.**

Romance, Inc.
Balance Sheet
January 4, 1996

#1	Cash	50,000			
	Fixed Assets (boat)	50,000	Common Stock	100,000
	TOTAL ASSETS	$100,000	TOTAL EQUITY	$100,000

(a) Assets (cash 50,000 + boat 50,000) increased by 100,000
    Equity (common stock) increased by 100,000

$$A = L + OE$$
$$100,000 = 0 + 100,000$$

(b) The owner(s) contributed 100,000 cash in exchange for 100,000 in common stock and then purchased a boat for 50,000 cash.

(c) Cash   100,000

          Common Stock 100,000

To record initial capitalization and issuance of stock for contributed capital (cash).

Boat   50,000

          Cash   50,000

To record the purchase of boat (gondola) for cash.

NAME:_____

Changes in Financial Statements: Pulling It All Together

Romance, Inc.
Balance Sheet
January 7, 1996

#2

Cash	35,000			
Prepaid Rent	9,000			
Prepaid Insurance	6,000			
Fixed Assets (boat)	50,000		Common Stock	100,000
TOTAL ASSETS	$100,000		TOTAL EQUITY	$100,000

(a)

(b)

(c)

Romance, Inc.
Balance Sheet
January 14, 1996

#3

Cash	50,000		Note Payable	20,000
Prepaid Rent	9,000			
Prepaid Insurance	6,000			
Fixed Assets (canopy)	5,000			
Fixed Assets (boat)	50,000		Common Stock	100,000
TOTAL ASSETS	$120,000		TOTAL LIAB. & EQUITY	$120,000

(a)

(b)

(c)

NAME:_____

Changes in Financial Statements: Pulling It All Together

Romance, Inc.
Balance Sheet
January 21, 1996

#4

Cash	50,000		Acct Payable	4,000
Office Supplies	1,500		Note Payable	20,000
Equip. (5 years)	2,500			
Prepaid Rent	9,000			
Prepaid Insurance	6,000			
Fixed Assets (canopy)	5,000			
Fixed Assets (boat)	50,000		Common Stock	100,000
TOTAL ASSETS	$124,000		TOTAL LIAB. & EQUITY	$124,000

(a)

(b)

(c)

Romance, Inc.
Balance Sheet
January 28, 1996

#5

Cash	50,000		Acct Payable	4,000
Office Supplies	1,500		Note Payable	20,000
Accts Receivable	16,000			
Equip. (5 years)	2,500			
Prepaid Rent	9,000			
Prepaid Insurance	6,000			
Fixed Assets (canopy)	5,000		Common Stock	100,000
Fixed Assets (boat)	50,000		Retained Earnings	16,000
TOTAL ASSETS	$140,000		TOTAL LIAB. & EQUITY	$140,000

(a)

(b)

(c)

NAME:_____

Changes in Financial Statements: Pulling It All Together

Romance, Inc.
Balance Sheet
January 28, 1996

#6

Cash	58,000		Acct Payable	4,000
Office Supplies	1,500		Note Payable	20,000
Accts Receivable	8,000			
Equip. (5 years)	2,500			
Prepaid Rent	9,000			
Prepaid Insurance	6,000			
Fixed Assets (canopy)	5,000		Common Stock	100,000
Fixed Assets (boat)	50,000		Retained Earnings	16,000
TOTAL ASSETS	$140,000		TOTAL LIAB. & EQUITY	$140,000

(a)

(b)

(c)

Romance, Inc.
Balance Sheet
January 30, 1996

#7

Cash	56,000		Acct Payable	2,000
Office Supplies	1,500		Note Payable	20,000
Accts Receivable	7,000			
Equip. (5 years)	2,500			
Prepaid Rent	9,000			
Prepaid Insurance	6,000			
Fixed Assets (canopy)	5,000		Common Stock	100,000
Fixed Assets (boat)	50,000		Retained Earnings	15,000
TOTAL ASSETS	$137,000		TOTAL LIAB. & EQUITY	$137,000

(a)

(b)

(c)

NAME:_____

Changes in Financial Statements: Pulling It All Together

Romance, Inc.
Balance Sheet
January 31, 1996

#8

Cash	56,000		Acct Payable	2,000
Office Supplies	1,500		Note Payable	20,000
Accts Receivable	7,000			
Equip. (5 years)	2,500			
Prepaid Rent	7,500			
Prepaid Insurance	5,000			
Fixed Assets (canopy)	5,000			
Accumulated Depr.	<958>		Common Stock	100,000
Fixed Assets (boat)	50,000		Retained Earnings	11,542
TOTAL ASSETS	$133,542		TOTAL LIAB. & EQUITY	$133,542

(a)

(b)

(c)

Extra Credit: What additional AJEs do you think should be made/considered at month's end?

Ashworth, Inc: Is Bigger Always Better?
Activity Overview

Why are we doing this activity?

The purpose of this activity is to enable you to convert verbal financial information into an accounting chart and then use the chart to compare and contrast growth in sales to changes in profits and, in turn, earnings per share. Many financial articles sound confusing to the average reader because of the treatment of the words "sales" and "earnings" as synonymous. They can mean the same, but earnings can also mean profits.

Content Goal:
* Compare growth in sales to changes in profits

Process Goal:
* Convert verbal financial information into an accounting chart

Activities Summary:

After reading the FACT SHEET on Ashworth, Inc., you will convert the information into a financial summary chart, then check and share your chart information with one of your teammates. Based on the chart, you will then respond to a set of questions about Ashworth's financial status (re: total sales and profits). Again you will share your responses with your teammate before a class discussion of Ashworth.

Activity Outcome:

When you have completed this activity, you should be able to apply an accounting structure to verbal information and help clarify the data being reported.

Class Discussion Notes:

Ashworth, Inc: Is Bigger Always Better?

Ashworth, Inc.
FACT SHEET

WHO: California corporation, located in Carlsbad, CA, fiscal year ending: 10/31/95

WHAT: Designs and manufactures golf apparel and sportswear

REPORT: (Financial Summary)

      "Ashworth, Inc. of Carlsbad, California reported increased sales but a slump in earnings for its fourth fiscal quarter and year ended October 31. The company recorded a fourth quarter loss of $2 million or 17 cents per share, on earnings of $13.1 million. A year earlier, Ashworth netted $133,126, or 1 cents per share on $11.6 in sales. For this year, Ashworth's net was $1.4 million, or 12 cents per share, on sales of $74.5 million. Last year, it earned $4.9 million or 40 cents per share on $60.8 million in sales."

Directions:

1. Read the short news brief, taken from the *San Diego Union-Tribune* of December 22, 1995.

2. Convert the financial summary into a comparison chart of years and quarters. An outline of the chart has been provided on the worksheet on the next page.

3. Answer the two questions posed at the bottom of the chart that are also on the next page.

4. Share your results with your teammate and check each other's responses.

NAME:_____
Ashworth, Inc: Is Bigger Always Better?

Use this worksheet to fulfill the requirements listed in the activity directions on the previous page (steps 2 and 3).

Date	10/31/95	10/31/95	10/31/94	10/31/94
Period	4th QUARTER	Fiscal Year	4th QUARTER	Fiscal Year
SALES				
INCOME or (LOSS)				
EPS				

1. Is bigger always better? Explain in the context of Ashworth's financial summary.

2. Do earnings and profits mean the same thing? Explain.

Accounts Receivable: House Accounts or on the House?
Activity Overview

Why are we doing this activity?

The purpose of this activity is to help you synthesize the business functions of credit policies, accounting for receivables and collection policies. Each of these functions is dependent on the others. Your ability to comprehend these interdependencies will increase your skill of using accounting concepts and information.

Content Goal:

* Use accounting concepts to interpret credit and collection policies

Process Goal:

* Improve listening skills by gathering information in an interview process

Activity Summary:

After you read the scenario facing Garibaldo's, a corner deli, you need to respond to the questions on the worksheet. You then need to interview one of your teammates for his or her responses. Take notes, so you can then share your partner's solutions with the class.

Activity Outcome:

When you have completed this activity, you should be able to integrate the need for credit policies, the use of accounting systems and the need for collection policies.

Class Discussion Notes:

Accounts Receivable: House Accounts or on the House?

You are the proud new owner of a local deli, Garibaldo's, situated in a great neighborhood. When you bought the deli, you also received an accounts receivable listing of customers who owed money to the deli along with a shoe box filled with slips of paper that contained the names of the "house account" customers. (These people all had charge privileges with the former owner of Garibaldi's.)

The former owner did not like computers or recordkeeping. He said he could spot a good credit risk by "a handshake and a look in the eye." Bills were not sent to house accounts as the former owner asked these customers to pay "when he needed cash flow and they (the customers) were in a good mood."

This is your first week of business and sales seem slow. Most of the activity comes at the lunch rush and many of your customers hurry in, grab stuff from the deli case and say, "Put it on my tab."

You think you need to make some changes, but you also don't want to make any of the customers mad.

Directions:

1. Read the scenario presented above and then jot down your responses to the three questions listed in the Interview Table on the next page.

2. Interview your teammate and record his or her responses in the column provided.

3. Switch roles and let your teammate interview you.

4. Report your **teammate's** responses back to the group.

NAME:_____
Accounts Receivable: House Accounts or on the House?

Use this grid to jot down your responses to the three questions listed and then to record the responses you get from the teammate you interview.

Question:	Your Response:	Teammate's Response
1. What are Garibaldi's current credit policies?		
2. How are accounts receivable recorded on the company books?		
3. What three changes would you make to the current way of doing business for Garibaldi's house accounts?	(a) (b) (c)	(a) (b) (c)

Checkbook Accounting: Cash vs. Accrual
Activity Overview

Why are we doing this activity?

The purpose of this activity is to build on your basic understanding of a checkbook (cash in and cash out) in order for you to be able to identify accrual accounting issues. Cash is usually the economic event that is recorded in the books, and then accrual accounting procedures are used to adjust cash reporting to accrual reporting. This activity starts with the known (cash) to help you use the new accrual accounting skills.

Content Goals:
* Compare and contrast cash and accrual basis
* Apply to a check-register situation
  and verify what changes need to take place

Process Goals:
* Combine creative and critical thinking
* Work independently and cooperatively

Activity Summary:

For starters, you will read the dilemma of a new business owner who is required to account for all of her financial activities to qualify for a special business start-up loan. After preparing a cash recap of her checkbook activity, you will also note what changes need to be made to convert the reports to an accrual basis. After trading and checking your teammate's responses, you'll then prepare a final accrual report to the loan committee along with a letter to the business owner explaining the accrual changes and recommending how she should keep her records in the future.

Activity Outcome:

When you have completed this activity, you should have a better understanding of the similarities and differences in cash and accrual accounting. You should also have improved your written and oral communication skills by working on your own reports and then critiquing a teammate's reports.

Class Discussion Notes:

Checkbook Accounting: Cash vs. Accrual

A good friend of yours needs your help. She has been selected to receive a "New Business" loan, because her business is located in a part of the city that needs business presence. She must provide the loan committee with an accrual basis report of her financial activity for the last month.

She has reviewed her checkbook and prepared a list of notes to help explain the check-register activity. (Both of these documents are on the following page.) The two things she wants you to do are (1) help her prepare an accrual report for the loan committee; and (2) explain to her how she can keep better records in the future.

Directions:

1. Prepare a cash basis balance sheet for 1995 (checkbook accounting). Use the worksheet on page 47.

2. Prepare the necessary adjusting entries to convert the cash reporting to accrual reporting Use the worksheet on page 47.

3. Draft a letter to your friend explaining why each adjustment was necessary and how she can keep better records in the future. REMEMBER, she is intelligent, but she does not have any accounting experience.

4. Trade papers with a teammate and check each other's responses. Discuss and resolve any differences.

5. Prepare a final set of reports to the loan committee, including an accrual basis Balance Sheet and Income Statement. Also prepare a final letter to your friend explaining the changes and what she should do differently in the future.

Checkbook Accounting: Cash vs. Accrual

Number	Date	Description	Payment	Deposit	Balance
	12/1	Start Up $$$		$10,000	$10,000
1001	12/1	RJ Mngmnt	$3,000		$7,000
1002	12/6	Staples	$500		
1003	12/6	Pacific Bell	$500		
	12/15	Deposit		$2000	
1004	12/15	Cost Co	$4000		
1005	12/18	State Farm	$450		
1006	12/18	Cost Co	$1250		
	12/24	Deposit		$2000	
	12/29	Bank Chrgs	$50		$6050

Notes about My Checkbook:

* I started my business with a $5000 loan from my parents and $5000 from my savings.
* I had to pay six months rent in December to my landlord, RJ Management.
* The phone company required a $500 deposit on my "800" number.
* My first order for SuperBowl baskets paid me a deposit of $2000 (orders have to be completed and shipped in January).
* I bought all the materials needed to make the baskets at CostCo on Dec. 15.
* I had to pay for three months of car insurance.
* I paid for the materials I needed to make 125 holiday baskets.
* I sold 100 holiday baskets.
* Bank charged me $35 for checks and a $15 service fee.

NAME:_____

Checkbook Accounting: Cash vs. Accrual

Garibaldi's
Balance Sheet - CASH BASIS
December 31, 1995

Cash   **Loans**

                                                    Owner's Equity

Total Assets $____   **Total Liabilities &**   ____
                                                    Owner's Equity $____

_____

Cash to Accrual Adjustments:

Date	Account	Debit	Credit

Inventory Decisions: Chocolates, Anyone?
Activity Overview

Why are we doing this activity?

The purpose of this activity is to help you master the cost flow assumptions used to record the value of inventory. This accounting valuation is a business tool that helps users of the inventory information make informed decisions about costs in relation to sales. The key concept in inventory valuation is to recognize that a pool of costs exists for all goods available for sale. Management's decision about an inventory method (LIFO, FIFO) does not change the costs in total; it only affects the flow of those costs to either the Balance Sheet (Inventory) or the Income Statement (COGS).

Content Goals:
* Compare and contrast LIFO with FIFO
* Distinguish flow of costs from flow of units

Process Goal:
* Use persuasion skills in presenting facts

Activity Summary:

You were elected treasurer and head of the ways and means committee for a campus organization, Phi Slamma Jamma. In reviewing the report and notes from last year, you found the club is the proud (?) owner of 500 candy bars from last year's fund-raiser. You also found out that another shipment was on the way! So your club is in the midst of another chocolate fund-raiser. Every club has to report to the university on its fund-raising activity. As the treasurer, you need to select an inventory method and explain to the club membership what it means and why it is the best method for the club to use.

Activity Outcome:

When you have completed this activity, you should have a better understanding of the similarities of the inventory methods as well as an appreciation for the strengths and weaknesses of each method. In addition, you should have a better awareness of the skills necessary to both present facts and persuade others.

Class Discussion Notes:

Inventory Decisions:　Chocolates Anyone?

"If I see another chocolate bar, I think I'll ..." As the new treasurer and head of ways and means for Phi Slamma Jamma, you are in the midst of the club's annual chocolate fund-raiser. "Why we keep trying to sell chocolates after last year's fiasco, I'll never know." When you took over as treasurer, you inherited a large supply of inventory as well as an order in process for more. Sales have been slow, but the club members look a little "rounder," so you suspect the sales force may be eating what it can't sell.

You just received a notice from the university requesting a report from the club on the status of its fund-raiser, including total funds collected, total costs of chocolate bars sold and total costs of bars unsold. Based on your recent accounting class, you know there are some decisions to be made, which can affect your report.

You've made a list of some key questions to discuss with the professor before you prepare the report to the university. Then you plan to prepare a short presentation to your club, explaining the report and the decisions you made as treasurer.

Directions:

1. Read through "Information Summary" that presents on the next page the facts concerning Phi Slamma Jamma's chocolate fund-raiser.

2. Based on the facts, the scenario explained above, and your knowledge of inventory valuations, briefly respond to the questions the treasurer has posed.

3. Discuss your answers with your team and resolve any differences. Be prepared to share your answers with the class.

4. Prepare a report for the university based on the requirements noted above.

5. Prepare a three minute presentation to Phi Slamma Jamma explaining which cost flow assumption you used and why it was best for the club.

NAME:_____

Inventory Decisions: Chocolates, Anyone?

Information Summary:

Chocolate bars purchased 5/12/95: 500 bars costing $200

Chocolate bars purchased 9/28/95: 500 bars costing $300

Sales of candy totaling $750. (Each bar sells for $1.25)

Candy bars remaining to be sold: 350 bars.

Questions to Be Resolved:

1. How should I report the "missing" candy bars?

2. What are the advantages to the club of using FIFO?   Disadvantages?

3. What are the advantages to using LIFO?   Disadvantages?

4. Will one method increase or decrease the amount of funds we raise?

Payroll Taxes: Who Pays More — Consultants or Employees?
Activity Overview

Why are we doing this activity?

The purpose of this activity is for you to comprehend the nature of payroll taxes for both employees and consultants (or people who are self-employed). Payroll taxes include federal and state withholding, but we will focus on the FICA tax and the Medicare tax, often referred to collectively as the Social Security tax.

Content Goal:
* Compare and contrast taxes for employees and self-employeds

Process Goal:
* Use numeric examples to explain verbal concepts

Activity Summary:

This activity places you in the role of an employee who is thinking about starting your own business, a consulting service advising companies how to prepare for OSHA safety inspections. You have decided to run your idea past your two best friends, but they have decidedly different opinions. You need to analyze the basic issue or dispute raised by the conversations and in turn sort out fact from fiction concerning the advantages and disadvantages of taxes for employees compared to self-employeds.

Activity Outcome:

When you complete this activity, you should have increased your comprehension of the facts regarding payroll taxes. Additionally, you should have strengthened your factual writing skills by using numeric information to help you summarize and explain a concept.

Class Discussion Notes:

Payroll Taxes: Who Pays More — Consultants or Employees?

You've been thinking of starting your own business as a consultant. You would provide advice and training for companies regarding OSHA safety regulations. That's what you do for the company you work for. And your boss has even "hinted" that the company gets a real bargain for your expertise.

You've heard of many advantages to being self-employed, but the big issue seems to be payroll taxes. In talking to your two best friends, they are both equally sure you should STAY an employee and START your own consulting service.

> Sam: "It makes a lot more sense to be a consultant because you get the gross amount of pay instead of just the 'take-home' amount."
>
> Jesse: "No way! A consultant has to pay <u>double</u> Social Security tax."
>
> Sam: "But consultants can deduct it, so they actually have LESS taxable income and more cash in the bank."
>
> Jesse: "Only in the short run ... Every April 15, they have to pay a bundle to the IRS!"

Directions:

1. Take each statement made by your friends and determine if it is FACT or FICTION. Use the grid on the next page.

2. Prepare a numerical example to prove the facts. Base the example on the information provided on the next page.

3. Trade papers with a teammate and see if your answers agree.

4. Discuss and resolve any differences.

5. Prepare a brief memo summarizing the FACTS about the FICA tax (Social Security tax) for employees and consultants. (A sample format is provided on page 54.)

NAME:_____

Payroll Taxes: Who Pays More — Consultants or Employees?

Fact or Fiction?

Statement	Fact or Fiction?	Explanation
"It makes a lot more sense to be a consultant because you get the gross amount of pay instead of just the 'take-home' amount."		
"A consultant has to pay <u>double</u> Social Security tax."		
"But consultants can deduct it (Social Security tax)..."		
"...so they actually have LESS taxable income and more cash in the bank."		
"Only in the short run ... Every April 15, they have to pay a bundle to the IRS!"		

Calculate an Example:

Base your calculation example on a weekly salary or consulting fee of $2,000, a FICA rate of 7.65 (.0765), and a self-employed rate of 15.3 (.153).

NAME:_____

Payroll Taxes: Who Pays More — Consultants or Employees?

MEMO TO:

FROM:

DATE:

SUBJECT:
======================================

Equity Valuations: Par, Book and Market Values
Activity Overview

Why are we doing this activity?

Wall Street (the major stock market) seems to play an ever increasing role in the average person's life, but many of its terms are not clearly understood by the average investor. This activity will help you discern the differences between three values assigned to stocks as well as the interrelationships between these values.

Content Goals:
* Recognize and state differences among stocks
* Discover relationships between these terms

Process Goal:
* Apply new concepts to "real world" terms

Activity Summary:

You have been asked to explain three stock terms to family members who have inherited some stock. The explanations need to include ideas and concepts, numeric examples and also some advice on the way the terms relate to each other. You will have an opportunity to draft your own set of responses and then discuss your responses in class.

Activity Outcome:

When you have completed this activity, you should have a stronger understanding of stock-value terminology as each term relates to the equity represented by stock ownership.

Class Discussion Notes:

Equity Valuations: Par, Book and Market Values

Your family is very proud of your college achievements, especially your track record in accounting. As the first member of your family to attend college, your relatives have started turning to you for explanations of many things.

Most recently your aunt and uncle have asked for your help in understanding the meaning of the information they have heard about stock values. As new shareholders of PepsiCo, resulting from an inheritance, they are both eager to learn and skeptical of what they know so far.

Directions:

1. Read through the list of questions on the next page posed by your relatives.

2. Respond to each question, using ideas and concepts, number examples and your accounting expertise to help them understand how these terms are applied to the same share of stock.

3. Be prepared to share these answers with the class.

NAME:_____
Equity Valuations: Par, Book and Market Values

To assist you in answering your aunt and uncle's questions, here is the most recent report of shareholders' equity in PepsiCo, for the year ended 12/31/95:

Shareholders' Equity (in millions, except per share amount)

Capital stock, par value 1⅔ cents per share; 1,800 shares authorized, 863 shares issued	$ 14
Capital in excess of par value	1,060
Retained earnings	8,730
Currency translation adjustment	(808)
	8,996
Less treasury stock, at cost, 75 shares	(1,683)
Total Shareholders' Equity	$7,213

NYSE quote for PepsiCo at high for 1995 = 58¾

1. How can my stock have three values? What is par, book and market value?

    par:

    book:

    market:

2. Which is the best value?

3. How does par value relate to book value?

4. How does book value relate to market value?

Business Consultation: Talking GAAP
Activity Overview

Why are we doing this activity?

  The purpose of this activity is to enable you to recognize accounting procedures used under Generally Accepted Accounting Principles (GAAP) and in turn explain HOW an entry is made as well as WHY such an entry conforms to GAAP. As a business consultant, you will practice three important skills in using accounting information: (1) explaining WHAT reinforces your verbal skills, (2) explaining HOW demonstrates technical skills, and (3) explaining WHY exercises your critical thinking skills.

Content Goals:
* Identify GAAP treatments
* Demonstrate accounting procedures
* Explain GAAP rationale

Process Goal:
* Integrate verbal, technical and critical-thinking skills

Activity Overview:

  This activity places you in the role of a family member/consultant. You need to gather information from the accountant and then recommunicate your findings to family members who have no business background and also think the accountant is not to be trusted. After drafting your own set of responses, you will compare your responses with your teammates. Based on your team discussion, you will come to a consensus on a final set of responses to share with the class.

Activity Outcome:

  When you have completed this activity, your understanding of GAAP concepts should have increased from three perspectives: WHAT, HOW and WHY. To add to your skills, you were able to practice coming to a consensus (one set of responses from the entire team) and sharing information with the large group (class).

Class Discussion Notes:

Business Consultation: Talking GAAP

A good friend of yours inherited the family business (a local grocery store) and just received a set of monthly financial statements (Balance Sheet and Income Statement). These were prepared by the same accountant who has done the accounting for years. Your friend has mailed the statements to you along with a letter expressing her concerns about certain items on the statements.

She's asking you to go to the accountant and find out what's wrong with the books. (The letter and statements are on the next pages).

Directions:

1. Read through the letter from Jack's friend Jill.

2. Using the statements supplied by the accountant, outline the key issues raised in each point in Jill's letter and the related GAAP treatment. Use the worksheet following the letter and financial statements.

3. Discuss your outline with your teammates and make any agreed-upon revisions.

4. Prepare a response to each issue raised in Jill's letter that explains how the entry was made and why it is correct. Use the FINAL worksheet on page 64.

Business Consultation: Talking GAAP

September 12, 1995

Dear Jack:

It was good talking to you yesterday. Can you believe the summer is over? Here are the copies of the reports on my family's grocery store I just received from the accountant. I sure need your help because I can never understand what those "bean counters" are trying to say.

I've put together a list of some issues my brothers have with what the accountant is doing. We think there may be some BIG problems with the books. Could you please talk to him and find out what's happening?

   1. What happened to the cash? How can we have net income and yet have the cash decrease? Is someone pocketing our cash?

   2. What about all the investments my father owned? I know he bought a variety of stocks with money he made from the business. Why don't any investments show up on these reports?

   3. I also know our store is located on very valuable property. The land was appraised at over $500,000 just six months ago. Why does the accountant only show it at $50,000? Did he just drop a "0"?

   4. One of the large expenses on the income statement is for depreciation, but we never authorized a check for that amount. And all our equipment is paid for, so this really looks bad.

   5. What about the mortgage owed to the bank? We make monthly payments of $750 and there are 10 years left to pay. The amount on the report is lower than the total remaining payments, so this needs correcting.

I have some other minor questions, but if you can get the accountant to fix these big mistakes (and find out if he even knows what he's doing), that would be a big help! Call me if you want to go over any of these in more detail. Again, thanks for being the go-between. (You were always so good at accounting!)

Your friend,

Jill

Business Consultation: Talking GAAP

ABC Grocery, Inc.
Balance Sheets
December 31, 1996 and 1995

	1996	1995
Cash	$125,000	$189,000
Accounts Receivable	90,000	100,000
Inventory	413,000	362,000
Prepaid Expenses	2,000	5,000
Total Current Assets	630,000	656,000
Property, Plant & Equipment	160,000	150,000
Less: Accumulated Depreciation	(130,000)	(110,000)
	30,000	40,000
Land	50,000	50,000
TOTAL ASSETS	$710,000	$746,000
Accounts Payable	$106,000	$260,375
Income Taxes Payable	58,500	23,625
Current Portion of Long-Term Debt	46,614	63,062
Total Current Liabilities	211,114	347,062
Long-Term Debt (Mortgage)	74,886	78,938
Total Liabilities	286,000	426,000
Common Stock	50,000	50,000
Additional Paid-in Capital	10,000	10,000
Retained Earnings	364,000	260,000
TOTAL LIABILITES & SHAREHOLDERS' EQUITY	$710,000	$746,000

Business Consultation: Talking GAAP

ABC Grocery, Inc.
Income Statements
For the Years Ended December 31, 1996 & 1995

	1996	1995
Sales	$948,000	$755,000
Cost of Sales	525,000	422,000
Gross Profit	423,000	333,000
Operating Expenses:		
Advertising	43,500	31,000
Depreciation	20,000	20,000
Legal & Accounting	10,000	9,000
Miscellaneous	1,500	2,000
Repairs & Maintenance	9,000	14,000
Salaries & Wages	148,500	158,000
Taxes - Payroll	22,000	23,875
Taxes - Property	6,500	9,500
Total Expenses	260,500	267,375
Income before Taxes	162,500	65,625
Provision for Taxes	(58,500)	(23,625)
NET INCOME	$104,000	$ 42,000

NAME:_____

Business Consultation: Talking GAAP

First Outline

Issue Raised:	GAAP Treatment:
1.	
2.	
3.	
4.	
5.	

NAME:_____

Business Consultation: Talking GAAP

Final Responses

Issue:	GAAP	HOW?	WHY?
1.			
2.			
3.			
4.			
5.			

Reading and Using Annual Reports: Financial Statement Analysis
Activity Overview

Why are we doing this activity?
The purpose of this activity is to help you synthesize many important aspects of accounting. Just as the title states, you will read and use financial information presented by a company in the form of an annual report. This activity helps you learn to gather information and be aware of the sources of information and then interpret, analyze and really use the information to evaluate a financial entity. Last but not least, this activity gives you practice in communicating your facts and analysis. Good fact-gathering skills are important, but the most important part of this activity is for you to be able to use facts to provide meaningful insights and comprehension of what the fact-patterns are indicating.

Content Goals:
* Understand the business
* Develop ratio analysis skills
* Understand the relationship between B/S, I/S and SCF
* Interprete financial statements
* Develop familiarity with industry analysis

Process Goals:
* Develop analytical skills
* Use business-writing skills
* Use presentation skills
* Evaluate information sources
* Integrate quantitative and qualitative information

Activity Summary:
This activity includes four separate but integrated parts and requires you to select a publicly traded coprporation to use in each part. You will need to gather information and prepare an analysis of your findings from three different perspectives: a short-term creditor, a long-term creditor and an investor. For the final report, you will be asked to assume the role of an employee of a fictitious company. Your findings in Parts A-C will then serve as the basis for Part D. You will need to incorporate the relevant aspects of each perspective for this final report, which is to help your "company" decide if the corporation you investigated would be a good customer. Your findings will be in both a written form (a three to five page report), and a brief presentation (five minutes), and should include at least one "picture" (visual aid).

Activity Outcome:
When you have completed this activity, you will have grown in your "work ethic," as this is a complex and challenging project. You will be better able to use financial statements to help you identify strengths and weaknesses of a company. You will also be aware that information has limitations, that numbers don't tell the whole story, that not all sources of information are equal, that questions are as important as answers, and that you can provide meaningful insights using good facts, not just accurate information that is "worthless."

Class Discussion Notes:

Reading and Using Annual Reports: Financial Statement Analysis
PART A - Liquidity

You are a credit analyst for a private company and have been assigned the task of preparing a credit analysis of a new customer. The analysis will include three parts, as noted below, and will be in the form of a Memo to the Files, which the head of your department will review.

Directions:

1. Obtain a copy of the Annual Report for your selected company. Read the financial statements, notes to the statements and Management Discussion sections.

2. Outline a draft of your memo and include the following sections in the body of the memo: Ratio Analysis section (the numbers and facts), Interpretation of Ratios (discussion of what the numbers and facts mean), and Recommendations (whether your company should grant credit to the new customer, and why or why not).

3. Calculate the ratios that indicate **Liquidity**, such as the Current Ratio, Quick Ratio, Net Sales to Working Capital, Receivable Turnover Ratio and Inventory Turnover Ratio. Prepare the ratios for the two most recent years (three if possible).

4. Analyze the ratios in terms of the trend over time (increasing, decreasing, fluctuating, etc.) and then explain what the trends might indicate. Explain what the numbers might be indicating based on the financial statements and your knowledge of accounting.

5. Prepare a MAXIMUM two-page typewritten memo reporting your findings, interpretations and recommendations. The following format is provided as a sample:

MEMO TO: Credit Files
FROM: Your Name
DATE: Due Date of Assignment
SUBJECT: Credit Analysis of "Company's Name"

First Paragraph: Introduction and scope of your report (what you will and will not cover)

Next Two to Four Paragraphs: Ratio Analysis section (the numbers and facts) and Interpretation of Ratios (discussion of what the numbers and facts mean). You may want to include your ratio calculations as an attachment to the memo.

Final Paragraph: Recommendations (whether your company should grant credit to the new customer, and why or why not).

Reading and Using Annual Reports: Financial Statement Analysis
PART B - Solvency

You are a credit analyst for a private banking group and have been assigned the task of preparing a long-term solvency analysis of a customer (company) that has applied for long-term financing from your bank. The analysis will include three parts, as noted below, and will be in the form of a Memo to the Files, which the head of your department will review.

Directions:

1.   Obtain a copy of the Annual Report for your selected company. Read the financial statements, notes to the statements and Management Discussion sections.

2.   Outline a draft of your memo and include the following sections in the body of the memo: Ratio Analysis section (the numbers and facts), Interpretation of Ratios (discussion of what the numbers and facts mean), and Recommendations (whether your company should grant credit to the new customer, and why or why not).

3.   Calculate the ratios that indicate **Solvency**, such as the Debt Ratio, Total Liabilites to Net Worth Ratio, and Coverage Ratio (times interest earned). Prepare the ratios for the two most recent years (three if possible).

4.   Analyze the ratios in terms of the trend over time (increasing, decreasing, fluctuating, etc.) and then explain what the trends might indicate. Explain what the numbers might be indicating based on the financial statements and your knowledge of accounting.

5.   Prepare a MAXIMUM two-page typewritten memo reporting your findings, interpretations and recommendations. The following format is provided as a sample:

MEMO TO: Bank Files
FROM: Your Name
DATE: Due Date of Assignment
SUBJECT: Solvency Analysis of "<u>Company's Name</u>"

First Paragraph: Introduction and scope of your report (what you will and will not cover)

Next Two to Four Paragraphs: Ratio Analysis section (the numbers and facts) and Interpretation of Ratios (discussion of what the numbers and facts mean). You may want to include your ratio calculations as an attachment to the memo.

Final Paragraph: Recommendations (whether your company should grant long-term financing to the new customer, and why or why not).

Reading and Using Annual Reports: Financial Statement Analysis
PART C - Profitability

You have recently inherited a large sum of money. After enjoying a brief, but intense, spending spree, you plan to invest $5,000 in a stock purchase of a publicly traded company. You have decided to prepare a profitability analysis of your prospective purchase. The analysis will include three parts, as noted below, and will be in the form of a Memo to the Files.

Directions:

1. Obtain a copy of the Annual Report for your selected company. Read the financial statements, notes to the statements and Management Discussion sections.

2. Outline a draft of your memo and include the following sections in the body of the memo: Ratio Analysis section (the numbers and facts), Interpretation of Ratios (discussion of what the numbers and facts mean), and Recommendations (whether you should invest in this company, and why or why not).

3. Calculate the ratios that indicate **Profitability**, such as Gross Margin, Before Tax Margin, Net Income, Return on Assets, Return on Equity, Earnings per Share, and Price-Earnings Ratio. Prepare the ratios for the two most recent years (three if possible).

4. Analyze the ratios in terms of the trend over time (increasing, decreasing, fluctuating, etc.) and then explain what the trends might indicate. Explain what the numbers might be indicating based on the financial statements and your knowledge of accounting.

5. Prepare a MAXIMUM two-page typewritten memo, reporting your findings, interpretations and recommendations. The following format is provided as a sample:

MEMO TO: The Files
FROM: Your Name
DATE: Due Date of Assignment
SUBJECT: Profitability Analysis of "Company's Name"

First Paragraph: Introduction and scope of your report (what you will and will not cover)

Next Two to Four Paragraphs: Ratio Analysis section (the numbers and facts) and Interpretation of Ratios (discussion of what the numbers and facts mean). You may want to include your ratio calculations as an attachment to the memo.

Final Paragraph: Recommendations (whether you should invest in this company, and why or why not).

Reading and Using Annual Reports: Financial Statement Analysis
PART D - Company Report

You are an employee of a successful accounting firm and have been asked to prepare a Company Report on a prospective new client for the firm. Your report will include relevant findings from the memos you completed in Parts A-C, but you will also need to include some additional research on **the industry** and **critical issues** facing the company. In addition to preparing a written report, you will also need to prepare a brief presentation of your recommendations.

Directions:

1. Obtain additional information about the company's industry. Robert Morse & Associates prepares key ratios by industry; Valueline prepares industry analyses. Work with the business librarian to locate references and to discover many on-line sources.

2. Obtain additional business-press articles about the company. Articles from *Business Week, Forbes, Fortune*, and the like.can provide a balanced perspective that may differ from what is reported by the company.

3. Draft a Company Report that includes the kind of coverage shown in the Sample Table of Contents below:

Sample Table of Contents

Executive Summary (2-3 paragraphs summarizing the report)

Company Background (2-3 paragraphs summarizing the company's products, services, length of time in business, size, major competitors, etc.)

Industry Trends (2-3 paragraphs explaining the industry)

Financial Analysis (sections covering Liquidity, Solvency & Profitability. MUST include Facts and Analysis in relation to the industry.)

Critical Issues (Identify and discuss two major issues facing the company based on article research: Competition, Regulation, Economy, Politics, Litigation, Public Concerns, etc.)

Summary and Conclusion (1-2 paragraphs recommending whether to accept this company as a new client, and why or why not.)

Reference List (at least five sources)

Attachments (Annual Report, Charts, Graphs, Ratios, etc.)

4. Prepare a brief (three to five minute) oral presentation of your recommendations.

Appendix A: Active Learning Structures

Reasoning Skills

Here are some "Tips" to help you develop your reasoning skills and your strategy for each activity. It's important to think about **the process** you use to complete a task. That process may be the same way you go about preparing other assignments, or it may be different, depending on the subject (**the content**). The most important aspect is for you to be aware of the process you use to reason and think, to think about your own thinking (the process), as well as to think about a particular subject (the content). Two important process skills in reasoning are described below along with some reasoning behaviors (questioning, organizing and connecting) and critical thinking reminders in the form of questions for you to use.

Skill 1: Develop Concept Formation- This skill requires you to categorize and group the details and procedures into bigger, related concepts.

Skill 2: Transform Abstract Descriptions into Concrete Outcomes- This skill requires you to take a concept/description and put it into action.

Reasoning Skills	What to Consider:
QUESTIONING	Do I understand the purpose? What are my assumptions? What is my point of view? What is the evidence?
ORGANIZING	Can I explain my choice of classifications? Can I give examples of differences? Can I give examples of similarities? Can I define how items relate?
CONNECTING	Can I link this information to my prior knowledge? Can I think of similar situations to describe this new knowledge (analogies)?

Think-Pair-Share[1]

Steps in the Process:

1. **Think:** Ponder the question being asked. Come up with your own solution.

2. **Pair:** Turn to a person next to you.

3. **Share:** Take turns talking and listening to each other.

OPTIONAL
4. **Square**: Pair with another pair to form a team of four.

Objectives and Rationale for Each Step:

THINK   Use this time to individually ponder the question and organize your thoughts. Try and solve the question by yourself and jot down areas you need explained. Many people need time to think alone before discussing questions. This time also helps you identify areas where you are stumped. The important skill you will practice is learning how to frame questions that get to the heart of what you need to have explained.

PAIR   Find someone sitting near you and form a pair. This step creates a miniteam of two. Having a partner can increase your confidence ("safety in numbers"), your problem-solving resources ("two heads are better than one"), and your comprehension ("teaching is learning").

SHARE   Actively use the time together and make sure you take turns talking and listening. Listening skills are in great demand but require lots of feedback between the sender and the receiver of the message. Learn to listen by suspending judgment and absorbing all the sender is giving. Use questions to make sure you are clear on what your partner is saying. Ask him or her to give examples, draw a diagram or whatever else it takes for you to clearly understand the message.

                Learn to give information by having a mental picture of what you are trying to explain. Use understandable terms, examples and analogies to help clarify what you are saying. Look for signals from the listener (facial gestures, body language, etc.) to help you adjust your message. Stop and ask for feedback -- for example, what do you think?

SQUARE   You can form an informal team of four by pairing with another pair.

---

[1]Lyman, F. 1981. "The responsive classroom discussion." In A. S. Anderson (ed.), *Mainstreaming digest*. College Park, Md.: University of Maryland College of Education.

Structured Problem Solving[2]

Steps in Process:

1. **Identify Roles:** Listen for your role assignment (a number, a card suit, a task).

2. **Ponder:** Organize your thoughts, locate your homework and individually get ready.

3. **Team Solution:** Team solves problem and reaches consensus on best answer.

4. **Report-Outs:** Be prepared for any team member to share results.

Objectives and Rationale for Each Step:

IDENTIFY ROLES You will take on various roles when you are a member of a team, so it is important to practice all roles (leader, recorder, spokesperson, monitor, etc.), rather than just stay with the ones you like. Even as a team member, you are still personally responsible for what you can produce as well as helping back up team members that may need help. This learning structure builds in individual accountability as well as team support.

PONDER It is always important to have our own thoughts and ideas. Some people think more quickly "on their feet," whereas others need time to reflect and prepare before sharing their ideas.

TEAM SOLUTION Many assignments will ask you to complete some portion of an activity outside class on your own. Then when the team works on a solution, you will need to consider all individual solutions and create the best team solution. This may require you to learn how to reach a consensus, as opposed to just "majority rules." Often the best solution is a combination of many individual parts that compels the group to a better product than any one individual could prepare.

REPORT-OUTS Most business-speaking situations require a skill known as impromptu speaking. This informal style is similar to class "report-outs." You need to be actively listening and participating during the team solution process so you can then share the results with others in the class (either the whole class or another team). Usually you will share your agreed-upon solution, but you may also be asked to share questions that you asked, areas of disagreement or the way you decided to approach the problem.

---

[2]Numerous sources, including Cottell, P. & Millis, B. 1992. "Cooperative learning in accounting," 10, *The Journal of Accounting Education, 95-111.*

Jigsaw[3]

Steps in Process:

1. **Pair:** Form an expert learning team based on card suits, numbering off or pairing.

2. **Prepare:** Expert team discusses and prepares how to teach its part of the problem.

3. **Teach:** Expert team members return to team and teach their part of the problem.

4. **Evaluation:** Team works together to make sure everyone understands all parts.

Objectives and Rationale for Each Step:

PAIR — Your task as a part of an expert team, whether it's a team of five or two, is to work together to first solve the problem or question you were assigned, and then develop strategies to teach this solution process to your base team. You are not just looking for the answer but, more important, you are working to share the "how to" process of getting the answer.

PREPARE — Working with this teaching process will help you diagnose what you don't fully understand (I can do it, but I can't tell you how), as well as increase your comprehension of what you know. As you work at preparing examples, giving pointers and outlining steps in the solution process (all where applicable), you will also gain an appreciation for the roles of student and teacher.

TEACH — Teaching requires active listening as well as presenting information. Develop a plan to use in presenting the "how to," which incorporates time for examples and feedback (questions, etc.) If you do all the talking, you may not know if "the students" comprehended the process.

EVALUATION — Once every team member has taken a turn teaching, then the team, as a whole, needs to make sure that everyone understands the entire process, not just one part of it. Ask a team member that wasn't "the expert" to explain one part. Then take turns and have each team member explain a part of the problem (BUT NOT THE SAME PORTION THE MEMBER TAUGHT!)

---

[3]Numerous sources, including Kagan, S. 1992. *Cooperative learning*. San Juan Capistrano, Calif.: Resources for Teachers, Inc.

Appendix B: Forming and Working in Teams

Cooperative Learning Overview Activity

Purpose: To help you comprehend certain basic elements of cooperative learning by becoming an "expert," preparing a strategy to teach certain concepts and teaching your teammates.

Directions:

If you are a Pair 1:

1. In the handout entitled "Basic Elements of Cooperative Learning" on the next page, read the sections about Positive Interdependence and Face-to-Face Promotive Interaction.
2. Pair with a partner and discuss how to teach the basic elements of Positive Interdependence and Face-to-Face Promotive Interaction.
3. When you are comfortable you know how to teach these basic elements, pair up with an adjacent Pair 2 and teach them.
4. When you are done, trade off and let the Pair 2 duo teach you.

If you are a Pair 2:

1. In the handout entitled "Basic Elements of Cooperative Learning" on the next page, read the sections about Individual Accountability/Personal Responsibility, Collaborative Skills and Group Processing.
2. Pair with a partner and discuss how to teach the basic elements of Individual Accountability/Personal Responsibility, Collaborative Skills and Group Processing.
3. When you are comfortable you know how to teach these basic elements, pair up with an adjacent Pair 1 and let them teach you.
4. When you are done, trade off and you teach the Pair 1 duo.

REQUIRED:
Within your group of four, make sure each member is clear on all of the five basic elements of cooperative learning. Use these elements as categories and provide examples of how to operationalize these elements.(See the worksheet on page 78.) Have the team recorder make notes of your results. Every team member should be prepared and able to present your examples to the class.

Cooperative Learning Overview Activity - Readings

Basic Elements of Cooperative Learning [4]

Students working together to get a job done in a classroom where students are concerned about each other's learning in addition to their own is the heart of cooperative learning. Cooperative learning is characterized by five basic elements:

Positive Interdependence exists when students believe that they are linked with others in a way that one cannot succeed unless the other members of the group succeed (and vice versa). Students are working together to get the job done. In other words, students must perceive that they "sink or swim together." In a problem-solving session, positive interdependence is structured by group members (1) agreeing on the answer and solution strategies for each problem (goal interdependence) and (2) fulfilling assigned role responsibilities (role interdependence). Other ways of structuring positive interdependence include having common rewards, being dependent on each other's resources or a division of labor.

Face-to-Face Promotive Interaction exists among students when they orally explain to each other how to solve problems, discuss with each other the nature of the concepts and strategies being learned, teach their knowledge to classmates, and explain to each other the connections between present and past learning. This face-to-face interaction is promotive in the sense that students help, assist, encourage and support each other's efforts to learn.

Individual Accountability/Personal Responsibility requires the teacher to ensure that the performance of each individual student is assessed and the results given back to the group and the individual. The group needs to know who needs more assistance in completing the assignment and group members need to know they cannot "hitch hike" on the work of others. Common ways to structure individual accountability include giving an individual exam to each student, randomly calling on individual students to present their group's answer, and giving an individual oral exam while monitoring group work.

Collaborative Skills are necessary for effective group functioning. Students must have and use needed leadership, decision-making, trust-building, communication, and conflict management skills. These skills have to be taught just as purposefully and precisely as academic skills. Many students have never worked cooperatively in learning situations and, therefore, lack the needed social skills for doing so.

Group Processing involves a group discussion of how well the members are achieving their goals and how well they are maintaining effective working relationships with each other. At the end of their working period, the groups process their functioning by answering two questions: (1) What is something each member did that was helpful for the group, and (2) What is something each member could do to make the group even better tomorrow? Such processing enables learning groups to focus on group maintenance, facilitates the learning of collaborative skills, ensures that members receive feedback on their participation and reminds students to practice collaborative skills consistently.

---

[4]From: Johnson, D. W., R. T. Johnson, and K. A. Smith. 1991. *Active learning: Cooperation in the college classroom*. Edina, Minn.: Interaction Book Co.

Cooperative Learning Overview Activity
Worksheet

Directions:

Use this worksheet to summarize, as a team, the best possible examples for each of the elements that are present in effective cooperative learning activities.

ELEMENTS:	EXAMPLE:
Positive Interdependence	
Face-to-Face Promotive Interaction	
Individual Accountability	
Collaborative Skills	
Group Processing	

Notes and Questions:

Team Structures: Best and Worst Experiences

Purpose: This activity is designed for you to analyze and dissect the best and the worst team experiences you have encountered. We can learn from nonexamples, i.e., how NOT to do something, as well as from examples. Most important, this activity will help you become aware of some key ingredients that are part of what makes for a good team experience.

Directions:

Structure
1.   Think back on team experiences you have had, particularly in the last year. Identify the best one and the worst one and jot them in the space provided below. Try and determine what made them the best and the worst by listing three telling signs.
2.   Briefly share the experiences with your team.
3.   Using everyone's experiences as a reference, study the table describing structures for teams on the next page and discuss which of the worst experiences might be improved by better structure.
4.   Prepare a checklist for your team to use in group activities for this class that will help provide the right kind of structure. Use the space provided in the table on the next page.

Participation
5.   Look at your notes on the best and worst team experiences. Are there any issues that have to do with participation?
6.   Discuss your views on participation **(attendance, effort, quality of contribution, level of cooperation)** and teamwork.
7.   As a team, agree on what will be acceptable levels of participation and give some concrete examples. Use the worksheet at the bottom of the next page.

Best Experience:

1.

2.

3.

Worst Experience:

1.

2.

3.

Team Structures: Best and Worst Experiences
Worksheets

Directions:

Use the first table to ponder the structural elements[5] listed as part of good team experiences. Then design a checklist for your team to use in deciding on how much structure affects teamwork in this course.

Structures for Teams

Team Structural Elements	Checklist
ORDER: How much or how little organization and orderliness are necessary?	
TIME: Are there time limitations? Is time allocated wisely to each part?	
GROUP SIZE: Does everyone get a fair share of work? Of time to share views?	
ATTITUDES: Are personality issues getting in the way of task issues?	
TASKS: Consider aspects of a task in deciding on the need for structure: how difficult, how interesting, how familiar, how much need for coordinated efforts.	

Participation Guidelines

Participation Element	Define the Element	Guidelines/Examples
Attendance		
Effort		
Quality of Contributions		
Level of Cooperation		

---

[5]Wilson, G. L. 1996. *Groups in context*. New York, NY: McGraw-Hill, Inc.

Team Minutes: Overview and Form
Overview

Minutes are similar to notes taken during lectures. The term *minutes* is the plural of minute and has as one of its meanings "the official record of proceedings of a meeting."[6] So you aren't literally keeping track of how many minutes your meeting lasted, although you may record when the meeting started and ended. Instead, you are taking notes of three main aspects: (1) who was present; (2) what was discussed and decided; (3) what will happen at the next meeting.

If you have ever been part of a club that requires minutes, you may think listening to the minutes being read is boring. The importance of minutes is to keep the members informed of what has been done and what remains to be done as well as who has agreed to do what. This recap or reminder is especially important on team projects or for those times when you can't remember what you agreed to do!

The form provided on the next page is a sample of one way to keep track of what was accomplished during team meetings. If you prepare and use an agenda for a meeting, the agenda can serve as a form to keep track of what happened. You also need to include notes of what is planned for the next meeting if the agenda doesn't have such a section.

The form is basic, but a few pointers are:

- Rotate the "Recorder" position.

- Take minutes at the time of the meeting (what the IRS calls "contemporaneous records"). If you forget to take minutes, then clearly state that you are reconstructing what happened from memory.

- Minutes can be brief but should be clear.

- Make sure you let the group know you need help in completing the minutes if the wrap-up goes too fast and you weren't sure who was doing what for future assignments and the like.

- It's usually a good idea to start a meeting by briefly reading or reviewing the minutes from last time. This helps everyone refocus on the tasks at hand. You can also correct the minutes if something is missing or not accurate.

---

[6] *Webster's Ninth New Collegiate Dictionary*. 1988. Springfield, Mass. Merriam-Webster Inc.

Team Minutes

Team #/Name:_____**Date:** _____

Recorder:_____

Members Present:

_____

Meeting Agenda: **(Items Discussed, Completed, Postponed)**

_____

Unfinished Business:

Assignments for Next Meeting: